D0741903

The Library of American Choreographers™

TWYLA THARP

Amelia Derezinski

rosen
central™

The Rosen Publishing Group, Inc., New York

Published in 2006 by The Rosen Publishing Group, Inc.
29 East 21st Street, New York, NY 10010

Library of Congress Cataloging-in-Publication Data

Derezinski, Amelia.
Twyla Tharp / Amelia Derezinski.— 1st ed.
   p. cm. — (The library of American choreographers)
 Includes bibliographical references and index.
ISBN 1-4042-0451-2 (lib. bdg.)
ISBN 1-4042-0646-9 (pbk. bdg.)
1. Tharp, Twyla—Juvenile literature. 2. Choreographers—United States—Biography—Juvenile literature. 3. Dancers—United States—Biography—Juvenile literature.
I. Title. II. Series.
GV1785.T43D47 2006
792.8'2'092—dc22

                                     2005006735

Manufactured in the United States of America

On the cover: Inset: A 1988 studio portrait of Twyla Tharp by Deborah Feingold/Getty Images. Background: Twyla Tharp (foreground) leads a dance class.

Contents

Introduction

With more than 125 dances to her credit, numerous awards, and thousands of adoring fans, Twyla Tharp has become one of the most successful choreographers in the world. Not only has she choreographed for her own company since 1965, but she has managed to create brilliant dances for Broadway, film, and television. Her creativity even extends to the world of writing—Tharp recently finished her second book!

Tharp has been inducted into the Academy of Achievement (a nonprofit organization dedicated to the education and inspiration of youth through the celebration of excellence in the achievements of Americans). In her interview with the academy, she described her motivation to excel in dance: "I thought I had to make an impact on history. It was quite simple. I had to become the greatest choreographer of my time.

Twyla Tharp (*right*) and Billy Joel join hands while receiving applause following the Broadway premiere of the dance musical *Movin' Out* on October 24, 2002. Drawing on Joel's extensive musical catalog, Tharp used his songs to craft a Vietnam-era coming-of-age story. This sad, joyous, angry, and inspiring story is told solely through Joel's lyrics and Tharp's choreography.

That was my mission and that's what I set out to do."

Twyla Tharp has certainly stayed true to her mission. After four decades of making dance and with many more creative and active years ahead of her, the legacy of Twyla Tharp—one of the greatest choreographers of her time—just continues to grow.

Twyla Tharp's Childhood and Education

"S he'll be famous, of that we've no doubt," wrote Mrs. Lecille Tharp announcing the birth of her daughter Twyla on July 1, 1941. From the moment Twyla was born, her mother prepared her to be a great artist. Even her name was chosen to ensure distinction. Mrs. Tharp changed the ordinary spelling of Twila with an "i" to Twyla with a "y," because she thought it would look better on a theater marquee.

Indiana

Twyla was born in Portland, Indiana, where her family lived until she was eight years old. Her parents, Lecille Confer Tharp and William Albert Tharp, both came from Quaker families who had been farming in Indiana for more than five generations. After earning their college degrees, Lecille and William married and moved off their families' farms and into town.

William Tharp owned a construction company and a Ford car dealership. He was known for his enormous energy, his ability to get things done, and his knack for building things from scratch, practical and creative traits Twyla definitely inherited. Having earned a degree in music, Twyla's mother taught piano to the local children. Lecille Tharp's love of music and belief that one can accomplish anything with hard work became driving forces behind Twyla's eventual success. Both Lecille and William encouraged Twyla to be the very best at everything she tried, a high standard that Twyla strove for and met throughout her life.

Twyla's artistic education began when she was still a baby, sitting on her mother's lap at the piano, listening and watching her mother play the music of all the great classical composers. When Twyla was only one and a half years old, her mother started giving her ear training, teaching her how to play the same notes on the piano that her mother was singing. When Twyla was four, Lecille Tharp realized that her daughter had true musical talent and sent her for piano lessons with a famous children's teacher.

All in all, Twyla and her three younger siblings, Stanley and Stanford (twin brothers), and her sister, Twanette, seemed to enjoy a happy childhood in Indiana. Then one day, her parents suddenly announced they would all be moving to Southern California, where her mother had bought a drive-in movie theater and her father another car dealership. Like in the days of the California gold rush, the Tharps would head west in search of their fortune. Besides, her parents reasoned, Twyla would now be closer to Hollywood where she could be "discovered" by someone with a keen eye for talent.

California Bound

None of the Tharp children wanted to leave Indiana. Nevertheless, in August 1949, the Tharps piled their children into the family car and embarked on their new life. Twyla Tharp tells the story of this cross-country trip in her autobiography, *Push Comes to Shove*: "We started driving, and I remember the flat landscape disappearing into a nothingness, an emptiness of which I am reminded every time I enter a studio and am enclosed by its blank walls." This uprooting from her home left Twyla with a restless spirit, memories to feed her choreography, and the sense that an empty studio means something new will be created.

William and Lecille set up their new businesses in

While the vastness of the open spaces found in the Great Plains and the American West can seem boring or empty to some people, Twyla Tharp found them inspiring. Something beautiful, startling, and fresh would emerge from her rich imagination to fill this seeming emptiness and blankness.

a small, dusty town called Rialto. The family lived nearby, in the foothills of Quail Canyon, a place surrounded by natural beauty. Twyla's father built their house by hand, a modern mansion complete with a playroom where Twyla could practice her many talents.

Twyla spent hours practicing the many lessons she had each week. Twyla's mother chose the best teachers within a hundred miles (161 kilometers) to provide Twyla with the finest training. Lecille drove more than 30,000 miles (48,280 km) a year to take Twyla to her lessons in ballet, toe (ballet performed wearing pointe shoes, so one can dance on the tips of one's toes), baton twirling, flamenco (a traditional dance from Spain), elocution (how to speak well), painting, viola, violin, drums, piano, cymbals, acrobatics, shorthand, German, and French.

Twyla's dance education began at the Vera Lynn Studio where she studied tap, toe, rope twirling, and Hawaiian dance. At age twelve, Twyla entered a new world of ballet training—a twice weekly, 200-mile (322 km) round-trip drive to study with Beatrice Collenette. Collenette had been taught by and performed with Anna Pavlova, one of the most famous ballerinas of the last 400 years! In her book *Push Comes to Shove*, Twyla describes her experiences taking classes with Collenette, "She also provided live music, not just records, played by a blind pianist whose melodies filled my body with a desire to express rhythms and emotions . . . So, of course, I understood that you play and dance by feel, not sight."

To fit all of these lessons in while still attending school, Twyla devised a strict schedule for herself.

Twyla Tharp (*far left*), Margaret Jenkins (*middle*), and Sara Rudner rehearse together. Rudner and Jenkins were important early members of Tharp's dance company. Both women would go on to form their own companies and become influential choreographers and teachers of dance in their own right.

She practiced two hours before school started, then continued with lessons after school until 8 PM. Not wasting a minute of time, Twyla did her homework by the light of the glove compartment in the car as her mother drove her to each lesson. She also "practiced" in the car, going over each routine in her head to imagine how she could execute a perfect performance.

College

After Twyla graduated from Pacific High School, she attended Pomona College in Claremont, California. She studied art history as her academic major. During her first semester, Twyla met her future husband, Peter Young. He was a visual artist and part of the avant-garde. Twyla's exposure to actual living artists helped her to challenge her own ideas about the art of dance and in what new directions it could be taken.

Strongly desiring to keep up with her early dance training, Twyla spent the summer after her freshman year in Los Angeles and took classes daily. Once in the hot spot of L.A., she studied with world-renowned dance teachers—ballet with Wilson Morelli, repertory with John Butler, and modern dance with Carmen de Lavallade and Bella Lewitsky.

During her second year at Pomona, Twyla was caught kissing her boyfriend in the college chapel—a serious violation of the college's strict rules. While this was one of Twyla's first acts of rebellion, it was certainly not her last. As a consequence,

Tharp's First Production

In Tharp's book *The Creative Habit,* she describes her first successful attempt at choreography when she was eight years old and living in Quail Canyon. She gathered together kids from around town and persuaded them to enter the back canyons with her. There she devised theatrical exercises for the children and directed them in a show of her own design.

Twyla Tharp and her dancers pose in the costumes they would wear for her piece *Generation*, presented at the Wagner College gymnasium on Staten Island, New York, on February 9, 1968. From left to right are Sara Rudner, Margery Tupling, Theresa Dickinson, Rose Marie Wright, and Tharp.

she was forced to transfer to another school. Her mother sent her to Barnard College, an Ivy League all-women's school affiliated with Columbia University. Barnard happened to be in the center of the dance world, New York City.

2 Dance Training in New York

How do you become one of the world's most famous choreographers? Being born with intelligence, talent, and a pushy mother is a good start. But what drove Twyla Tharp into the spotlight was a lifetime of training and, most important, practice, practice, practice!

Learning Dance from the Masters

In New York, Tharp continued her studies in art history, but she spent more of her time in the professional dance schools around the city, where she took two to three classes a day in ballet, jazz, and modern dance. Barnard College allowed Tharp to fulfill her physical education requirement with these outside classes, and she jumped at the chance to study with the best dance teachers. Two of these were Richard Thomas and Barbara Fallis, with whom she studied ballet. Thomas and Fallis were directors of the New York School of Ballet. Through their classes, Tharp was able to master fast and intricate footwork and learn how to manipulate dance phrases, skills that later became features of her own choreography.

Throughout her four years of college studies, Tharp debated what to pursue as her career. "I was coming to define myself as a dancer, much as I fought off the discovery," admits Tharp in *Push Comes to Shove*. She knew that it was very difficult to make a living as a dancer, and she feared the false but then common stereotype of "dumb" dancers and athletes.

However, Twyla Tharp's will to dance won out over her fears. Dancing was the thing she could do best and enjoyed more than anything else. In her book *The Creative Habit: Learn It and Use It for Life*, Tharp describes the moment she made her ultimate choice, the choice that changed her life and the history of dance forever: "I was a senior alone in a dressing room, next to a dance studio . . . I looked at my body in the dressing room mirror and, in that moment, I saw the potential for a dancer. As I was changing into practice clothes, I felt as if I were putting on a uniform, and I thought, 'Yes, I want to join this team.' That's when and how I made my life choice."

Merce Cunningham, a modern dance choreographer, photographed in September 1957, four years after he founded the Merce Cunningham Dance Company.

Ballet was just the beginning. Tharp was hungry for all kinds of dance and went "shopping" for the right modern dance teachers. She attended every dance concert she could find, including those of the leading choreographers of the time—Martha Graham, Merce Cunningham, Alvin Ailey, Erick Hawkins, Murray Louis, Jean Erdman, and many more. In her autobiography *Push Comes to Shove*, Twyla explains how she chose her teachers, "Watching each, I asked myself one question over and over: 'Is this how I should be dancing?' To address this question I studied with over half of these choreographers. Two have stayed with me particularly: Martha Graham and Merce Cunningham."

Tharp started taking modern dance with Martha Graham in 1961. What Tharp seems to have taken from her studies with Graham is the level of dedication she witnessed in Graham's studio. Tharp felt honored to be in a class with other dancers who were so committed to one another and to the work.

Once a Graham dancer himself, Merce Cunningham also contributed to Tharp's modern dance education. Unlike Martha Graham's choreography, Cunningham's dancers do not represent characters in a story. He is more interested in abstract movement than in dance telling a story. In fact, Merce Cunningham is credited with pioneering a whole new way to structure choreography. He often chooses the dance's sequence of movements by using chance—a toss of the coin can determine the order of the movement phrases that make up his dances.

Tharp rounded out her ballet and modern dance education with jazz. She studied with Eugene Lewis (a jazz dance leader known professionally as "Luigi") and admits that jazz was the most fun. In *Push Comes to Shove*, Twyla describes how studying jazz completed her education by ". . . adding the life and bounce . . . of show biz to the graceful elegance of classical ballet and the self-righteous rigor of modern dance."

Dancing for Paul Taylor

Dance, eat, and sleep. That was Twyla Tharp's life in her early twenties. She was dedicated to training her body, the instrument of her art. She even skipped her college graduation to attend rehearsal with Paul Taylor, a major figure in the modern dance field. He would be the final choreographer Tharp worked with and trained under as a dancer before setting out on her own.

In 1963, Tharp landed the opportunity to work with him simply by insisting on it. "I just walked in . . . I

Members of the Paul Taylor Dance Company perform a modern dance piece in London, England, in November 1964. Though based in New York, the company was performing its first London season at the Shaftsbury Theatre, in the city's West End theater district.

chose him, he certainly didn't choose me. I just started hanging out at his studio, more or less refusing to leave," remembers Tharp in *Push Comes to Shove.*

Tharp's feisty spirit earned her a professional job dancing in Paul Taylor's company. However, it wasn't long before Tharp started to question Taylor's movement choices as he made his dances. She felt like his dances were becoming mere entertainment, not art, and that possibly she could do better. She was beginning to form her own vision of what dance should be but did not yet have the confidence to leave Taylor's company. She needed to get fired in order to receive the necessary push into her own career as a choreographer. In the fall of 1964, Taylor overheard Tharp criticizing his work to a well-known dance critic from the *New York Times,* Clive Barnes. Shortly thereafter, Taylor called Tharp into his office and suggested that she try going out on her own.

On Her Own

Tharp wanted to keep dancing, but she didn't quite know how. She auditioned all over the city for jobs she didn't really feel were right for her, including commercials, industrials (corporate events), and showgirl routines. She even auditioned for the Radio City Rockettes, who loved her technical abilities, but couldn't she please just smile while she performed her high kicks? In *The Creative Habit*, Tharp describes her growing realization that she would just have to create dance for herself. "Finally, between rounds of auditions, interviews, and unemployment lines, I could stall no longer. If I was going to dance, I was going to have to learn the lesson Ruth St. Denis had taught Martha Graham and which Martha had once shared with me: 'I went in and Miss Ruth said, 'Show me your dance.' 'I don't have one,' Martha replied. Miss Ruth responded, 'Well dear, go out and get one.'" And that is just what Twyla Tharp did.

3 Twyla Tharp at Work

To the question, "What is dancing?" Tharp's answer is, "I allowed myself only one assumption: dance is movement in space and time" (as quoted in *Push Comes to Shove*). Tharp's first choreographed dance was called *Tank Dive*. According to *Push Comes to Shove*, the title referred to Tharp's feelings about her chances of making it big, ". . . like diving from a very high platform, about nine hundred thousand feet up, into a thimbleful of water."

Tank Dive

The time was April 29, 1965, and the place was room 1604 at Hunter College in Manhattan. The room was actually a studio in the art department where her husband, Robert (Bob) Huot, was an instructor. She describes this seven-minute piece in *Push Comes to Shove*, "I began in the dark with almost nothing . . . entering upstage of the audience. The ending was face down, in a blackout, an homage to death: how else to end definitively?" Needing to decide on the middle, she chose what she felt were the most elemental movements—the circle, the spiral, the right angle, and the diagonal. Four nondancers, including Huot, performed alongside Tharp in this premiere performance.

Tharp's dramatic costumes were designed by her husband (who designed all the costumes for Tharp until 1970). Tharp began in a backless leotard, red bell-bottoms, and velvet high-heeled bedroom slippers. She then stepped out of the slippers and into a pair of large wooden shoes that looked like fat skis. Jennifer Tipton designed the lighting, the first project of a lifelong collaboration with Tharp.

Judson Church

No critics reviewed *Tank Dive*, and in fact, not many critics reviewed her dances for the next four years. This was actually a fortunate circumstance for the young choreographer. She learned to develop her own unique style and vision, without being influenced by other people's suggestions or criticisms. She made art only for herself, not for the approval of critics or the pleasure of audience members.

Twyla Tharp (*left*) rehearses her dance *Eight Jelly Rolls* in 1975. At right is Sara Rudner, who danced in Tharp's company from 1965–1985.

Taking her ideas into the studio, Tharp then collaborated with her dancers Margaret Jenkins and Sara Rudner in defining an aesthetic, or distinctive visual and artistic style. They rehearsed four hours per day, six days a week, at the Judson Church gym where many older, avant-garde choreographers also rehearsed and performed. These choreographers favored experimentation using everyday movements that anyone could perform. "At the Judson you could only walk and run—if you danced you had sold out," recounts Tharp in *Push Comes to Shove*. Tharp's style was different than that of other Judson choreographers. Tharp's dancers had to draw upon their technical abilities to execute her choreographed movements that combined difficult modern dance movements with ballet and jazz.

Tharp stuck to her beliefs and presented two dances at Judson Church, which Clive Barnes of the *New York Times* called "bad in a rather interesting way" (as quoted in *Push Comes to Shove*).

Defining a Style

Following the modest success of the Judson Church dances and a brief European tour, Tharp continued to define her style in her New York studio. In *Push Comes to Shove*, Tharp describes her groundbreaking approach to movement: "Gradually I began asking questions about counterpoint: where were the harmonies and tensions of movement? . . . We inverted phrases, turning movements upside down, flexing instead of extending the feet . . . We learned to retrograde movements, running them backward, like film images in reverse . . . Slowly our style—too balletic to be modern, too modern-dance to be ballet, too everything for the Judson—which had first won us enemies, was beginning to earn critical appreciation."

In 1969, Tharp received numerous favorable reviews for her piece *After Suite*. This indicated that she was on the path of success. Deborah Jowitt of the *Village Voice* wrote approvingly, "She has been able to do what I thought might be impossible; she has transferred her own incredible style to her company. This style—speaking very super-ficially—involves acquiring a strong classical technique and then learning to fling it around without ever really losing control. The dancing is difficult, quirky, beauti-ful, stylish" (as quoted in *Push Comes to Shove*).

In 1970, Tharp created *The Fugue*, a dance that amazed audiences with its complex movement inspired in part by mathe-matics. Tharp's other major inspiration was Johann Sebastian Bach's *Musical Offering*, which uses twenty variations on a twenty-count theme. Dancers perform these variations by reversing, inversing, and resequenc-ing the original, initial movements. However, the dancers do not perform with Bach's accompani-ment. Instead, they make the music themselves with their footsteps beating rhythms in stack-heeled boots on an amplified stage.

Tharp earned critical acclaim for this beautifully complex work. In *Ballet Review*, Arlene Croce said of the dance, "*The Fugue* might as well stand for the quintessential Tharp dance. Basic Tharp body move-ment—the spiraling twists and off balance lunges and kicks, the shuffles and stomps that look exclu-sively hers." *The Fugue* has now entered into modern dance's classic repertoire, and its intricate movements and variations continue to draw people into its intelligent and elegant patterning.

That's Entertainment!

The year 1971 marked a shift in the aesthetic of Tharp's choreography and the company itself. Pregnant with her son, Jesse, Tharp acknowledged that she would soon be sitting in the audience watching, instead of dancing on stage. She began to choreograph with the audience's enjoyment in mind more than her own pleasure as a dancer. This was a big departure from the work of her peers and from her own philosophy of the previous six years that art existed with or without an audience, and the viewers' needs and pleasure did not need to be considered.

For the first time in her career, Tharp began to choreograph to music—1927 jazz tunes by Jelly Roll Morton. The result was *Eight Jelly Rolls*, with choreography that entertained using humor, virtuosity, and jazz style. This piece marked a new collaboration between Tharp and fashion and lighting designers, placing the company at the vanguard of style. Costume designer Kermit Love changed the "poor artist" aesthetic of the company to a more chic look by dressing the dancers in form-fitting, sleeveless and backless tuxedos. Stylist Vidal Sassoon also gave

Legendary jazz pianist Jelly Roll Morton appears in this autographed 1915 photograph. Morton grew up in New Orleans, Louisiana, and learned the piano by age ten. While working as a wandering pianist throughout the South, he developed his distinctive jazz style that combined ragtime, blues, religious hymns, and gospel.

the company a new look with fashionable haircuts, far different from the company's bohemian beginnings. Jennifer Tipton designed the lighting, which added to the highly polished aesthetic.

Blending Dance Styles in *Deuce Coupe*

In 1973, Robert Joffrey, director of the Joffrey Ballet, asked Tharp to create a piece for his company. The resulting work, *Deuce Coupe*, was a blending of two separate dance worlds—the pop culture of 1960s social dance with the high arts of ballet and modern dance—and audiences fell in love with it. For the piece, Tharp choreographed her company of modern dancers alongside the more classical Joffrey dancers, a first in the history of modern and ballet performances. As she recounts in *Push Comes to Shove*, the new piece *Deuce Coupe* was a way to reclaim her past: "Along with the proprieties of the ballet, I would blend a vernacular [common or popular] style composed of running, skipping, sliding, and tumbling, plus all those magical steps [from popular dances] I never did—the bugaloo, the mashed potato, the slop, the go-go—the whole of this funneled through a little bit of Broadway show biz via the authentic energy and personalities of my dancers."

For *Deuce Coupe*, Tharp chose songs by the Beach Boys, music that reminded her of Southern California. Composer David Horowitz then blended these songs into the soundtrack. Her inspiration for *Deuce Coupe*'s set design came to her from the graffiti sprayed on New York City subway cars. For each performance, she had six street kids create a new spray-painted mural upstage, while the dancers danced. Fashion designer Scott Barrie made hip and casual costumes: bright orange dresses for the women, and yellow-green pants for the men topped with Hawaiian print shirts. The lighting, designed by Jennifer Tipton, was characterized by shadows, patterns, colors, blackouts, and silhouettes.

Tharp's combining of the established, classical dance form of ballet with popular dancing, street art, and pop music was a huge success.

Working with Misha

American Ballet Theatre (ABT) was the next premier ballet company to hire Tharp. Although she went on to choreograph for ABT for fifteen years, her first work for them, *Push Comes to Shove* (1976), remains the most well-known. She was hired to choreograph a ballet that would feature Mikhail (Misha) Baryshnikov, a Soviet defector to the United States and one of the most famous male ballet dancers of all time.

Like the two distinct American and Russian cultures, embodied by the collaborators, the music also represented a duality as Joseph Lamb's early jazz mingled with Franz Josef Haydn's classical music. Tharp choreographed movements to show off Baryshnikov's unsurpassed Russian ballet technique and created the character of an irresistible, flirtatious, American-style boy in this ballet for one man and sixteen women.

Baryshnikov and Tharp enjoyed this first collaboration so much that they went on to work on several projects together in the years to come. *Baryshnikov by Tharp*, an Emmy Award-winning TV special for the

Public Broadcasting System (PBS) debuted in 1984. One year later, the film *White Nights* was released. Starring both Baryshnikov and tap legend Gregory Hines, the film features Tharp's dynamic dance sequences for these two dance legends. Tharp and Baryshnikov were drawn together again in 1993 for *Pergolisi* (a solo work for Baryshnikov with costumes by fashion designer Isaac Mizrahi) and a duet for Tharp and Baryshnikov entitled *Bare Bones*. At this point, Tharp was fifty-two years old and still dancing strong!

Film

After watching *Push Comes to Shove*, film director Milos Forman invited Tharp to choreograph for his 1979 film *Hair*. Wanting to learn more about film directing and yearning for stardom on the screen, Tharp agreed to this all-consuming project. *Hair* is adapted from an earlier musical of the same title and is concerned with the troubled lives and difficult decisions of American youth at the time of the Vietnam War. Twyla Tharp's choreography injects vibrant life into the film, including army sergeants dancing while seated at a table, policemen's horses tapping their hooves in time to the music, and a dancing hippie tribe frolicking in Central Park. Tharp and Forman collaborated on later projects as

Twyla Tharp (*left*) and Mikhail Baryshnikov take a break during rehearsals for the American Ballet Theatre's production of *Push Comes to Shove* in 1975. This was one of Tharp's early "crossover" dances in which she mixed ballet and more popular dance styles. *Push Comes to Shove* features classical ballet steps as well as looser, more experimental movements.

well, with Tharp providing choreography for Forman's films *Ragtime* (1981) and the Oscar-winning *Amadeus* (1984).

Amid these film shoots, Tharp managed to travel back and forth between an expanding variety of projects, many of them with world-class athletes. In 1976, Tharp created *After All* for Olympic gold medal–winning figure

Mikhail Baryshnikov (*left*) and American tap dancer Gregory Hines dance together in this film still from the 1985 movie *White Nights*, directed by Taylor Hackford. Twyla Tharp provided the choreography for the film's dance sequences.

skater John Curry. This ice-ballet changed the look of figure skating, giving more attention to detailed qualities of movement as opposed to sequences of skills and jumps. In 1980, Tharp again worked with Curry, making the piece *Three Fanfares* as part of the closing ceremonies of the winter Olympics. In that same year, she also choreographed *Dance Is a*

Man's Sport Too, an (ABC) Omnibus television special featuring Pittsburgh Steelers wide receiver Lynn Swann and New York City Ballet principal dancer Peter Martins.

Broadway

Twyla Tharp was not content with choreographing for major motion pictures, the finest ballet companies in the world, her own successful modern troupe, and Olympic and professional athletes. Ever ambitious and creatively restless, she decided to choreograph and direct her own original Broadway shows. Her successful Broadway debut was in 1980 at the Winter Garden Theater, in New York City, with *When We Were Very Young*. This dance-theater piece named for a poem by A. A. Milne (the creator of Winnie the

Twyla Tharp has provided the choreography for five major Hollywood films, including three directed by Milos Forman: *Amadeus* (1984), *Ragtime* (1981), and *Hair* (1979). A film still from *Hair* appears above. One of the main characters, a hippie named George Berger (Treat Williams), has crashed a high society party and disrupts the fancy luncheon by jumping on the dining room table and dancing raucously. While dancing, he sings a song that celebrates his freedom, vitality, and uninhibited love of life.

Pooh) was based on problems Tharp had in her own life balancing her career with her role as a mother.

Only one year later, she tried her hand at Broadway again, this time in a collaboration with pop music icon David Byrne of the band Talking Heads. Their theme for the production, *The Catherine Wheel*, was a sensation that they discovered they had both shared as children—that of feeling separate from their family. As Byrne composed the music, Tharp choreographed short sections, each no longer than a minute long. Although the production lost money, *The Catherine Wheel* became the subject of a British television documentary, and Tharp once again gained a larger audience for her work through collaborating with other artists and by combining a range of art forms with modern dance.

In 1985, Tharp directed and choreographed the Broadway adaptation of the 1952 movie-musical *Singin' in the Rain*. Famed tap dancer Gene Kelly choreographed the original movie, and, in a rare act of humility, Tharp kept most of his choreography intact. Despite this, audiences and critics preferred the original film to Tharp's stage version.

With her ever-growing number of experiences,

skills, and talented collaborators to draw upon, Tharp's fourth attempt at choreographing for Broadway proved to be an astounding success. *Movin' Out* premiered at the Richard Rodgers Theatre on October 24, 2002. Conceived, directed, and choreographed by Tharp, this dance-play tells the story of high school friends as they deal with the trials of love and the tragedies of war.

Tharp began her research for this production with the songs of Billy Joel. She decided to create a single, continuous story using the characters in his songs and set the action in the time of the Vietnam War (the late 1960s to early 1970s). She then did research about that time period—she read newspapers, watched television dance shows of the time, and studied the era's clothing styles. With all of this information swirling in her mind, Tharp went in the studio to improvise. What she came up with was a brilliant work in which the story is told through dance and music only. There is no dialogue, but the narrative is clearly and emotionally conveyed through the dancers' movements and Joel's lyrics.

Movin' Out was a critical success and a popular smash. Among other awards, it received the Vietnam Veterans of America President's Award and

Cast members of *Movin' Out* perform a scene from the Broadway musical during the fifty-seventh annual Tony Awards at Radio City Music Hall in New York City on June 8, 2003. The show won two Tony Awards. Twyla Tharp won one for Best Choreography, while Billy Joel and Stuart Malina were awarded a Tony for Best Orchestrations. It received ten Tony nominations, including Best Musical. The Tony Awards are presented each June by the American Theatre Wing and the League of American Theatres and Producers to honor distinguished achievement in Broadway theater.

the highest honor on Broadway, the Tony Award. The show continues to play to sold-out audiences both on Broadway and throughout the country thanks to a touring production.

4 Twyla Tharp's Legacy

Before Twyla Tharp ever made her first dance, she considered how hard it would be to create a lasting impression or legacy through an art form whose pieces cease to exist after the curtain closes. In her book *The Creative Habit*, Tharp explains her determination to forge ahead despite the fear of impermanence: "Our creations disappear the moment we finish performing them. It's tough to preserve a legacy, create a history for yourself and others. But I put all that aside and pursued my gut instinct anyway." Despite her fears, Twyla Tharp has created and continues to create a tremendous legacy in dance.

Innovation

For the past forty years, Twyla Tharp has been making dances her own way. She reintroduced technically virtuosic (or difficult and masterful) dance to the concert stage. In doing so, she faced the accusation from the avant-garde that she was selling out. Even today, following her success with *Movin' Out*, Tharp is accused by some in the dance world of catering to popular tastes.

When Tharp was beginning to forge her characteristic aesthetic (or look and style), no other choreographer for the concert stage was blending so many different techniques as she was. She used her eclectic (or wide and varied) training to make something original, melding ballet, modern, tap, and popular dance elements into a unified style. Because her pieces incorporate so many influences and techniques, Tharp's dancers have to be as varied in their training as Tharp herself is. They also must possess lightning-quick brains to keep up with her complex movent variations and mathematical phrasing.

Tharp's Living Legacy

Tharp's legacy is ensured both through the continued performance of her work and through her creative influence on future generations of dancer-choreographers. Each new dancer who learns Tharp's repertoire keeps her choreography alive within his or her body. Tharp dancers retain a "muscle memory" of Tharp's technique and style and continue her legacy with each performance.

Tharp's legacy is also built upon and preserved when her dancers go out and choreograph their own works or teach in schools and studios throughout the world. A family tree of dance is created, in which Tharp is the trunk and her former dancers are the branches. Some of Tharp's dancers who have gone on to teach or choreograph their

Twyla Tharp and her dancers perform in *Sue's Leg* for the inaugural episode of PBS's *Dance in America* . A tribute to American music and dances of the 1930s, Tharp drew on the songs of pianist and jazz composer Fats Waller and the dance style of tap legend Bill "Bojangles" Robinson. From left to right are Rose Marie Wright, Tom Rawe, Tharp, and Kenneth Rinker.

own dances are Rose Marie Wright, Tom Rawe, Jennifer Way, Shelley Washington, Christine Uchida, Raymond Kurshals, Richard Colton, Anthony Ferro, William Whitener, John Carrafa, Katie Glasner, John Malashock, Mary Ann Kellogg, Shelley Freydont, Keith Young, Kenneth Rinker, and Sara Rudner.

Award-winning productions require collaboration with designers, and Tharp has worked with the best in the business. Two of her most long-term collaborators are lighting designer Jennifer Tipton and set, costume, and production designer Santo Loquasto. Tipton has designed lighting for Tharp since her first dance, *Tank Dive*, in 1965, and has worked on more than seventy-five of her pieces. Loquasto has worked with Tharp since 1975, collaborating on more than fifty works, including the recent Broadway success *Movin' Out*. Tipton has become the top name in lighting design for dance and has earned numerous awards for her work, including two Bessie Awards (the highest prize in modern dance) and the Dorothy and Lillian Gish Prize, worth $250,000. Loquasto has won six Tony awards and eight Drama Desk Awards for his work in theater. More recently, he has been a production designer in film and has worked with the famous

Awards and Accomplishments

- First-ever PBS's *Dance in America* show featuring Tharp's work, *Sue's Leg*
- Seventeen honorary doctorates
- Chicago International Film Festival Award for *Making Television Dance*, which she coproduced and codirected
- Tony award for *Movin' Out*
- Drama Desk Award & Outer Critics Circle Award for Outstanding Choreography for *Movin' Out*
- Vietnam Veterans of America President's Award for *Movin' Out*
- Astaire Award for *Movin' Out*
- Drama League Award for Sustained Achievement
- National Medal of Arts (awarded by the president of the United States to artists who have made extraordinary contributions to the creation, growth, and support of the arts in the United States)

director Woody Allen on numerous movies.

Tharp has also worked with famous designers from the fashion world adding glamour to the company image. These designers include Ralph Lauren, Oscar de la Renta, Norma Kamali, Gianni Versace, and Isaac Mizrahi. World-renowned celebrity photographer Richard Avedon captured Tharp and her company in many photos over the years. These exquisite black and white photos

Twyla Tharp stands between opera composer Carlisle Floyd (*left*) and U.S. president George W. Bush in the Oval Office of the White House on November 17, 2004. She and Floyd had just received the 2004 National Humanities Medal and the National Medal of Arts for their lifetime contributions to American art and culture.

helped push Tharp's career forward in the 1980s and have captured the essence of Tharp. The Avedon photographs have created for Tharp and her company a legacy of images.

A Legacy Preserved

Although live performances end when the curtain closes and can never be recaptured, Twyla Tharp has worked to express her creativity and preserve her work in more permanent ways. To date she has written two books. Her first book is her autobiography, *Push Comes to Shove*, published in 1992. It is a fascinating account of her life and the creative process by which many of her dances were made. Her second book, *The Creative Habit: Learn It and Use It for Life*, instructs readers on how to incorporate creativity into everyday life. It is filled with Tharp's secrets of success in making a career out of creativity. Tharp's crossover work in video, film, and photography has also ensured a rich and enduring record of her works.

Since her debut in 1965, Twyla Tharp has created more than 125 dances, and she's still going strong! She has made dances for her own company and for the Joffrey Ballet, American Ballet Theatre, New York City Ballet, Paris Opera Ballet, the Royal Ballet, Hubbard Street Dance Theater, and the Martha Graham Dance Company. Tharp has choreographed for film and television, collaborated with pop music stars, and won numerous awards, including the Tony Award and the National Medal of Arts. She is known throughout the world of dance as a master choreographer and will go down in history as one of the best.

Tharp's greatest accomplishment, however, is her own satisfaction. Despite the long odds of being able to make a living, much less make history, as a dancer-choreographer, Tharp followed her dreams, and her daring has been rewarded. At this point in her career, Twyla Tharp is able to declare that becoming a dancer was the best idea she has ever had.

Glossary

avant-garde A French word literally meaning "advance guard." It is often used to describe artistic movements concerned with new and often shocking ideas that are generally not popular at the time they are introduced.

improvisation The act of experimenting or thinking and acting on the spot.

jazz A term describing a general category of dance performed to popular or jazz music. There are many different styles of jazz dancing.

legacy The lasting impression a person's life makes on succeeding generations; the influence or inheritance a person passes along to those who come after him or her.

modern dance A style of dance that developed in the early part of the twentieth century in Europe and America. Stylistically, early modern dance was generally performed barefoot, often to percussion music. Today, it is known as a type of dance that is reinvented by each choreographer with the idea being to discover new ways of expression through the body.

movement phrase A brief sequence of movement that has a distinct beginning, middle, and end.

repertoire All the dances that a company or individual performs.

For More Information

Twyla Tharp Dance Company
710 10th Avenue #2
New York, NY 10011
(212) 333-4751
Web site: http://www.twylatharp.org

Web Sites

Due to the changing nature of Internet links, the Rosen Publishing Group, Inc., has developed an online list of Web sites related to the subject of this book. This site is updated regularly. Please use this link to access the list:

http://www.rosenlinks.com/lac/twth

For Further Reading

Cutcher, Jenai. *Gotta Dance!: The Rhythms of Jazz and Tap*. New York, NY: The Rosen Publishing Group, Inc., 2004.

Derezinski, Amelia. *Star Turns: Dancing on Broadway*. New York, NY: The Rosen Publishing Group, Inc., 2004.

Kessel, Kristin. *Dance Performance: From Rehearsal to Opening Night*. New York, NY: The Rosen Publishing Group, Inc., 2004.

Mitchell, Missy. *Ballet: Pointe by Pointe*. New York, NY: The Rosen Publishing Group, Inc., 2004.

Tharp, Twyla. *The Creative Habit: Learn It and Use It for Life*. New York, NY: Simon & Schuster, 2003.

Bibliography

American Dance Festival. "Twyla Tharp." Undated. Retrieved July 2004 (http://www. americandancefestival.org/Archives/ scripps/tharp.html).

Danceworks Online. "Twyla Tharp Biography." Retrieved August 2004 (http://www. danceworksonline.co.uk/sidesteps/people/ tharp.htm).

Levin, Jordon. "Still Getting Her Kicks: Twyla Tharp." *Los Angeles Times*, September 22, 1996.

Mackrell, Judith. "Uptown Girl." *Guardian*. June 2003. Retrieved July 2004 (http://www. guardian.co.uk/arts/features/story/ 0,11710,987624,00.html).

"Profile: Twyla Tharp." Academy of Achievement-A Museum of Living History. Undated. Retrieved July 2004 (http://www.achievement.org/autodoc/ page/thaObio-\).

Smiley, Tavis. "Interview: Twyla Tharp Discusses Creativity." *Columbia Encyclopedia*, 2004. Retrieved July 2004 (http://www.encyclopedia. com/html/t/tharp-t1w.asp).

Tharp, Twyla. *The Creative Habit: Learn It and Use It for Life*. New York, NY: Simon & Schuster, 2003.

Tharp, Twyla. *Push Comes to Shove*. New York, NY: Bantam Books, 1992.

"Twyla Tharp: Biography, Company Archives." Twyla Tharp Dance Company. Retrieved July 2004 (http://www.twylatharp.org/ttl.shtml).

Index

About The Author

Amelia Derezinski has been choreographing and dancing professionally in New York City since 1996. Ms. Derezinski earned her M.A. in dance and dance education from New York University and teaches dance to children and adults. Ms. Derezinski's first book, *Star Turns: Dancing on Broadway*, was published by The Rosen Publishing Group in 2004.

Photo Credits

Cover © Deborah Feingold/Getty Images; cover (back), pp. 23, 31 © Gjon Mili/Time Life Pictures/Getty Images; p. 5 © AP/Wide World Photos; p. 9 © David Stoecklein/Corbis; pp. 11, 13, 39 © Jerome Robbins Dance Division, The New York Public Library for the Performing Arts, Astor, Lenox and Tilden Foundations; p. 16 © Charles E. Rotkin/Corbis; p. 18 © Hulton-Deutsch Collection/Corbis; p. 27 © Time Life Images/Getty Images; pp. 32, 33, 48 © Columbia Pictures, Courtesy Everett Collection; p. 36 © Frank Micelotta/Getty Images; p. 42 © Brendan Smilalowski/AFP/Getty Images.

Designer: Tahara Anderson
Developmental Editor: Nancy Allison, CMA, RME